Waleed Wakes Up

Mini Mu'min Du'a Series #17

www.Mini-Mumin.com

Copyright © 2012 Mini Mu'min Publications

All rights reserved. This publication may not be reproduced in whole or in part by any means whatsoever without written permission from the copyright owner.

Introduction

All praise is due to Allah the Most High, may Allah send His blessings on the Prophet Muhammad (saw), his family, his companions, and those who follow him in righteousness until the Day of Judgment.

"And remember your Lord by your tongue and within yourself, humbly and in awe, without loudness, by words in the morning and the afternoon, and be not among those who are neglectful." (Holy Qur'an 7:205)

The **Mini Mu'min Du'a Series** is designed to help you teach your child essential Islamic supplications and the situations in which they would be used. Each book focuses on a single topic, with key vocabulary **highlighted**. These key words can then serve as a tool to remind your child of important points. All supplications are shown in Arabic text, translation, and transliteration. For any assertions regarding fiqh we have provided textual proofs, from the Qur'an and authentic Sunnah of the Prophet (saw), at the bottom of the relevant page. Each story is accompanied by original artwork, but in accordance with Islamic beliefs we do not use human or animal images.

Transliteration has been provided here as a means to help those who do not know Arabic to teach supplications to their children. But it must be noted that all transliteration is imperfect and cannot accurately represent Arabic sounds in their entirety. We therefore encourage anyone who uses our books to use the transliteration as a tool, but not an end in itself, and to eventually learn the supplications in the original Arabic.

In some cases, sounds will be represented in the transliteration (because they are present in the Arabic text) that will not actually be pronounced. These generally occur at the end of a supplication and are related to the Arabic rules for pausing and stopping. To clarify this for non-Arabic speakers, we have placed brackets [ ] around those sounds in the transliteration that would not be pronounced when reciting the supplication.

Thank you for purchasing this book, may Allah benefit both you and your child through it, forgive us for any errors we have made, and benefit us in this life and the Hereafter if there is any good in it.

The sky above is dark,
But the stars are sparkling bright.

The world below is sleeping,
Through the long and peaceful night.

The full moon shines down gently
With its soft silvery beams,

On Waleed's quiet little town
And all their sleepy dreams...

The night is filled with soft sounds,
Like the croaking of the frogs,

And the bubbling of the brook
Past their lily pads and logs.

The crickets in the tall grass,
Chirping their evening song,

Fill the night with their lullaby
Singing sweetly all night long…

In a little red farmhouse
At the top of a rolling hill,

In his soft and warm bed,
Waleed is sleeping still…

On a fluffy white pillow
His sleepy head rests,

Like a bird snuggling down
In its warm and cozy nest.

The night is almost over,
Its job is nearly done,

The day is slowly coming,
With the rising of the sun…

As the light spreads out,
The birds chirp and cheer!

The world is waking up,
Morning is almost here…

Suddenly, the alarm clock rings-
Time to get out of bed!

Waleed opens his eyes,
As he slowly scratches his head.

With a twist and a stretch,
And a wiggling of toes,

Waleed sits up and looks around,
Rubbing his small nose...

Does Waleed get right up
And play with all his toys?

No, that's not the thing to do
For Muslim girls and boys…

Does Waleed get right up
To go and watch T.V.?

No, there is something else
More important to do, you see...

Does Waleed get right up
And eat a tasty tart?

No, he has a much, MUCH,
Better way to start!

When Waleed gets up
Each and every day,

He has something special
That he likes to say…

Waleed always remembers
The **du'a** that we make,

In the early morning,
Right away, **when we wake**.

الْحَمْدُ لِلَّهِ الَّذِي أَحْيَانَا بَعْدَ مَا أَمَاتَنَا وَ إِلَيْهِ النُّشُورُ

"Alhamdu lillaahil-la__th__ee ahyaanaa ba'da maa amaatanaa wa ilaihin-nushoor"

(Praise be to Allah who gives us life after He has caused us to die and unto Him is the return.)[1]

---

[1] Al-Bukhaari with Al-Fath 11/113 and Muslim 4/2083

From **Allah** we **come**,
And to **Allah** we will **return**,

In **sleep** and **waking**
There are lessons that we learn.[2]

Waleed always remembers
Allah when he wakes,

For giving him the gift of **life**,
While other souls He takes.

---

[2] "It is Allah that takes the souls (of men) at death; and those that die not (He takes) during their sleep: those on whom He has passed the decree of death, He keeps back (from returning to life), but the rest He sends (to their bodies) for a term appointed verily in this are Signs for those who reflect." (39:42)

After Waleed's special du'a
For waking had been said,

He made wudoo' and Fajr[3] prayer-
Then he neatly made his bed.

Waleed was very happy,
And his smile was very bright,

Because he knew just how,
To start his day out right!

---
[3] "Fajr"- One of the five daily prayers in Islam.

Waleed looked out his window,
At the brand new dawning day,

If a Muslim knows his ad'iyaa[4]
He always knows just what to say!

Do you know your du'a?
Have you learned it yet?

Just make sure, when you do-
That you don't forget!

---
[4] "Ad'iyaa"- Arabic word meaning "supplications" (plural form of the word "du'a").

The End!

Other available titles in the Mini Mu'min Du'a Series:

Batool's Bedtime Story
Bilal's Bakery
Fatimah's First Fasting Day
Jameelah Gets Dressed
Muhammed Goes to the Masjid
Sheema's Shopping Spree
Saliha Sneezes
Waheeda the Wudoo' Wonder

and many more!...

Visit our online bookstore at:

www.Mini-Mumin.com

Made in the USA
Charleston, SC
13 January 2014